Dear Parents and Educators,

Welcome to Penguin Young Readers! As parents and educators, you know that each child develops at his or her own pace—in terms of speech, critical thinking, and, of course, reading. Penguin Young Readers recognizes this fact. As a result, each Penguin Young Readers book is assigned a traditional easy-to-read level (1–4) as well as a Guided Reading Level (A–P). Both of these systems will help you choose the right book for your child. Please refer to the back of each book for specific leveling information. Penguin Young Readers features esteemed authors and illustrators, stories about favorite characters, fascinating nonfiction, and more!

Pouch Babies

LEVEL **3**

GUIDED
READING
LEVEL **M**

This book is perfect for a **Transitional Reader** who:
- can read multisyllable and compound words;
- can read words with prefixes and suffixes;
- is able to identify story elements (beginning, middle, end, plot, setting, characters, problem, solution); and
- can understand different points of view.

Here are some **activities** you can do during and after reading this book:
- Compare/Contrast: This book talks about many different marsupials. Pick one marsupial from each chapter and compare and contrast them. How are they alike? How are they different?
- Nonfiction: Nonfiction books deal with facts and events that are real. Talk about the elements of nonfiction. Then make a list of what you learned in this nonfiction book. For example, red kangaroos can hop up to 40 miles per hour. See how many facts you can find!

Remember, sharing the love of reading with a child is the best gift you can give!

—Bonnie Bader, EdM, and Katie Carella, EdM
  Penguin Young Readers program

To my mom, Karen Hamilton, for showing me how to be a nurturing and encouraging mother—GLC

Penguin Young Readers
Published by the Penguin Group
Penguin Group (USA) Inc., 375 Hudson Street, New York, New York 10014, USA
Penguin Group (Canada), 90 Eglinton Avenue East, Suite 700, Toronto, Ontario M4P 2Y3, Canada (
a division of Pearson Penguin Canada Inc.)
Penguin Books Ltd., 80 Strand, London WC2R 0RL, England
Penguin Group Ireland, 25 St. Stephen's Green, Dublin 2, Ireland (a division of Penguin Books Ltd.)
Penguin Group (Australia), 250 Camberwell Road, Camberwell, Victoria 3124, Australia
(a division of Pearson Australia Group Pty. Ltd.)
Penguin Books India Pvt. Ltd., 11 Community Centre, Panchsheel Park, New Delhi—110 017, India
Penguin Group (NZ), 67 Apollo Drive, Rosedale, Auckland 0632, New Zealand
(a division of Pearson New Zealand Ltd.)
Penguin Books (South Africa) (Pty.) Ltd., 24 Sturdee Avenue,
Rosebank, Johannesburg 2196, South Africa

Penguin Books Ltd., Registered Offices: 80 Strand, London WC2R 0RL, England

Illustrations by Lucia Washburn.

Text copyright © 2011 by Ginjer L. Clarke. Illustrations copyright © 2011 by Lucia Washburn.
All rights reserved. Published by Penguin Young Readers, an imprint of Penguin Group (USA) Inc.,
345 Hudson Street, New York, New York 10014. Manufactured in China.

Library of Congress Cataloging-in-Publication Data is available.

ISBN 978-0-448-45107-7   10 9 8 7 6 5 4 3 2 1

Pouch Babies

by Ginjer L. Clarke
illustrated by Lucia Washburn

Penguin Young Readers
An Imprint of Penguin Group (USA) Inc.

quoll

What is a marsupial? Most mammal babies are born helpless. But they can move around without their mother soon after they are born.

Marsupial (say: mar-SOO-pee-ul) babies are not like other mammals. When marsupial babies are born, they are no bigger than beans! The babies grow bigger while tucked safely inside their mothers' pouches. Marsupials can grow to be as small as mice or as big as adult humans. Marsupials include koalas, kangaroos, quokkas, quolls, and many other animals.

Most marsupials are nocturnal. That means they are awake at night and asleep during the day.

Here is a quokka mother with her baby. A quokka is like a small kangaroo.

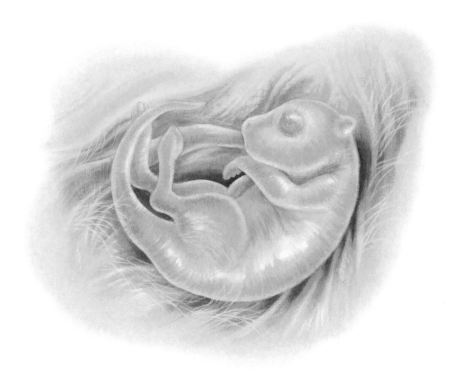

Most marsupial mothers keep their tiny babies safe in pouches. The mother's pouch opens from the front near her belly or the back near her tail, depending on how she moves.

Kangaroos give birth to one baby at a time. A baby kangaroo is called a joey. The joey is hairless and blind.

The **gray kangaroo** mother licks her belly fur to make a trail. The joey follows it into the pouch. It drinks her milk for several months. The pouch protects the joey from being hurt or eaten by dingoes or foxes. Let's find out more about marvelous marsupial mammals!

Chapter 1
Kangaroos and Wallabies

Kangaroos live in Australia. **Red kangaroos** are the largest of all the marsupial mammals. Males can be as much as six feet tall when they sit up on their tails. Female red kangaroos are smaller and more blue-gray than red. *Boing! Boing!* Red kangaroos can hop up to 40 miles per hour and jump over 40 feet of land in a single bounce!

A red kangaroo joey stays in its mother's pouch for six months. It hops out now and then to explore. Then the joey goes back into the pouch to sleep. It dives headfirst into the pouch and twists around until its head, feet, and tail stick out. The joey stays safe inside the pouch.

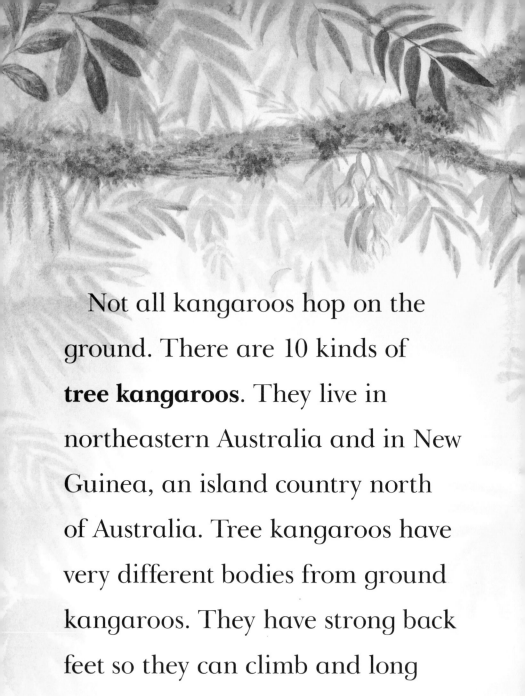

Not all kangaroos hop on the ground. There are 10 kinds of **tree kangaroos**. They live in northeastern Australia and in New Guinea, an island country north of Australia. Tree kangaroos have very different bodies from ground kangaroos. They have strong back feet so they can climb and long front feet with claws to hold on to branches.

Pounce! Some tree kangaroos can leap up to 50 feet between branches! Their extra-long tails help them balance. Mother and baby jump in the trees, eating leaves, flowers, and fruit. The tree kangaroo joey stays in its mother's pouch for up to one year. Hang on tightly, little tree kangaroo!

Rock wallabies are related to tree kangaroos and can be found all over Australia. The rock wallaby can climb over boulders, cliffs, and ledges. It has thick pads on its back feet to help it cling to the rocks.

Yellow-footed rock wallabies live in large groups of about 50 to 100. They eat grass, leaves, and roots that they find in the rocks. The rock wallaby joey stays in its mom's pouch for only a few weeks. It has to learn how to find food quickly because it is on its own from a young age. Good luck, little wallaby!

The **pademelon** (say: PAD-eh-MELL-un) is a very small wallaby that lives in the forests of Australia and New Guinea. Pademelons are not good jumpers. They use their strong front feet to push through bushes to make paths. They use these paths when they go out at night to find berries, leaves, and grass to eat.

The pademelon mother and joey are looking for food in the forest. Suddenly, they hear something. *Thump! Thump!* The pademelon stomps the ground twice with her feet. If the animal thumps back, she knows it is just another pademelon nearby. If not, she and her baby will hide. *Thump! Thump!* No worries this time.

western hare wallaby

spectacled hare wallaby

The **hare wallaby** is the smallest member of the kangaroo family. It is only the size of a small rabbit, but it can leap up to 25 feet. The hare wallaby mom carries her joey in a front pouch like other wallabies. The **spectacled hare wallaby** lives in the forests of northern Australia.

The **western hare wallaby** is rare.
It only lives on two islands near
Australia. The western hare wallaby
is also called a whistler because
it squeaks when it senses danger.
Squeak! The western hare wallaby
mother dashes for cover under
a bush.

Chapter 2
Koalas, Wombats, and More

Koalas live in eastern Australia. Eucalyptus (say: yoo-kuh-LIP-tis) leaves are the only food the koala eats! So the koala spends most of its life in the tops of eucalyptus trees.

The koala baby stays in its mom's backward-facing pouch for six months. Then it rides on its mother's back.

Koalas look cuddly, but they will
bite and scratch others to keep their
babies safe. They can use their big
toes like human thumbs to hold
on to trees. Koalas sleep curled
up in the fork of a tree during the
day. *Smooch!* This koala kisses and
snuggles her baby to sleep.

Common wombats look like a cross between a small bear and a badger. They live in southern Australia. Like koalas, the wombat mother has a backward-facing pouch. The baby wombat peeks out of it while its mom digs for food. Dirt stays out of the pouch.

Wombats eat grass at night and
sleep underground during the day.
After a long night of digging, the
mom and baby wombat curl up in
their cozy den for a nap. G'day,
wombats!

The **Tasmanian devil** lives only
in Tasmania (say: taz-MAY-nee-uh),
an island south of Australia. *Screech!*
The Tasmanian devil screams
at night when it hunts. These
screams scared the people who
first discovered the animal, so they
called it a Tasmanian devil. The
Tasmanian devil has sharp teeth,

but it is usually shy around people.

Baby Tasmanian devils stay in their mother's backward pouch and drink her milk for four months. Then the devil mom cuddles her babies in a den during the day. They will each grow to be about the size of a small dog by nine months old. What darling little devils!

The **Tasmanian tiger** looks like a dog with a wolf's head and a tiger's stripes. This crazy creature used to live in Tasmania, all over Australia, and in New Guinea, but it is now extinct. The last Tasmanian tiger died in a zoo in 1936.

The Tasmanian tiger was about four feet long and was a meat eater. It hunted kangaroos, birds, and other animals. The Tasmanian tiger mother carried her cubs in a backward pouch until they were big enough to hunt. Some people think Tasmanian tigers are still alive, but no one can prove it.

The **numbat** is the size of a squirrel. It lives in Western Australia. It is also called a banded anteater, but it eats more termites than ants.

The numbat scratches open a termite nest with its claws. *Slurp!* The numbat pulls termites out with its long, sticky tongue.Numbats can eat up to 20,000 termites in one day!

Numbats are the only marsupials that eat mostly during the day. The numbat mother does not have a pouch like most marsupials. Her babies start out tiny. They stay stuck tightly to her belly and drink her milk for a few months. Then she hides them in a nest inside a log until they are six months old.

Chapter 3
Opossums and Possums

The **Virginia opossum** is the only marsupial found in Canada and the United States. The opossum eats fruit, insects, eggs, small animals, and trash. Opossums have long tails that are prehensile (say: pre-HEN-sul). This means their tails curl around and tightly hold on to branches.

The opossum mother can give birth to as many as 20 tiny babies. Each baby is so small that they could all fit into a teaspoon! The babies grow quickly in their mother's backward pouch. After they are 10 weeks old, they sleep together in a nest. Mom lets them ride piggyback when she hunts for food at night.

Many other smaller opossums live in Central and South America. There are nine different kinds of **mouse opossums**. They can see and hear well, and they are good hunters. Mouse opossums eat insects, spiders, lizards, and some fruit.

Like numbats, mouse opossum moms do not have pouches for their babies. A newborn mouse opossum is not much bigger than a grain of rice! These tiny babies hang on to the fur between their mother's back legs. Later, the babies cling to their mom's back as she crawls along a branch.

brush-tailed possums

Some other Australian marsupials are called possums, but they are different from American opossums. The **brush-tailed possum** lives in the forests of Australia and New Zealand. It has a bushy tail and thick fur that can be black, brown, silver, or gold.

The brush-tailed possum mom has one baby that grows in her front pouch. After it is five months old, the baby holds tightly to its mother's back. The mother uses her tail to steer. *Wheee!* They leap across treetops at night, eating fruits, flowers, and even some birds' eggs.

The **striped possum** is also called a skunk possum because it has black-and-white stripes and smells like a skunk. It lives in the treetops of rain forests in Australia and New Guinea. The striped possum's baby stays in her pouch for two months. Then it rides on her back.

striped possum

skunk

The striped possum eats mostly
insects that live in tree trunks and
rotten logs. *Tap! Tap!* The striped
possum mom taps a log with her
front feet. She rips the bark with
her teeth. Then she sticks her long
fourth toe into the tree and grabs
a bug. She slurps it up with her
tongue. What a tasty bug snack!

The tiny **honey possum** is about the size of a mouse and has a pointy snout. It weighs the same as three nickels. It lives in the fields and grasslands of southwestern Australia. The honey possum drinks nectar from flowers like a hummingbird. Its long tongue has a scratchy tip to help it suck up the sweet liquid.

The honey possum mom keeps her babies in her pouch for two months. Then she leaves them in a nest while she drinks from flowers. She keeps feeding her babies her milk. When they are five months old, they go on flower-feeding trips. Honey possums are small and sweet!

Chapter 4

Miscellaneous Marsupials

The **cuscus** (say: koos-koos) looks like a mix between a sloth and a monkey, but it is really a possum. The cuscus can be orange, white, gray, or brown, and some males have spots on their backs. It moves slowly through the treetops of New Guinea and northern Australia. It sleeps sitting up during the day.

The cuscus likes to be alone. The mother cuscus protects her baby in her front pouch. *Bark! Bark!* She sees another animal and warns it to stay away from her. When she feels safe again, she goes back to munching leaves. But she always watches out for trouble.

The **greater glider** is the largest of the flying marsupials. It lives in Eastern Australia. It has a flap of skin that stretches from its elbow to its knee. The greater glider uses this flap like a sail and floats from tree to tree. *Whoosh!* A greater glider can leap to a tree up to 300 feet away. That is almost the length of a football field!

A greater glider mom and her baby can make a perfect landing in the dark. Gliders have large eyes and ears that face forward so they can see and hear in the dark. The greater glider baby stays in its mother's pouch for about four months. Then the glider baby holds on to its mom's back as they fly through the trees, munching on eucalyptus leaves.

The **potoroo** is also called a rat
kangaroo. There were ten kinds of
rat kangaroos, but seven of them
are now extinct. The **long-footed
potoroo** has a tail and body like a
rat, but it has long feet and hops
like a kangaroo. It lives only in
one small part of southeastern
Australia. It is in danger of
becoming extinct.

The potoroo eats mostly funguses, but it also likes insects and plants. It feeds at night on the forest floor.

The potoroo mother carries her baby in her front pouch for four months. Then the baby leaves the pouch and hops around with its mother. If the baby wanders away, its mom calls out using a low, kissing sound to tell the baby to come back.

There are 22 kinds of **bandicoots**.
They weigh from one to ten pounds.
Some have long noses or long ears.
They live in the forests, plains,
and deserts of Australia and New
Guinea. **Long-eared bandicoots**
can hear well. When the bandicoot
hears a noise, it jumps straight into
the air. *Zip!* Then it turns and runs
away.

The **long-nosed bandicoot** mom
holds her babies in a backward
pouch. She often has new babies
before the older ones are ready
to leave. About four older babies
and four tiny, new babies squeeze
in together. That is one crowded
pouch!

The **marsupial mole** lives in the deserts of central Australia. People have rarely seen this mole, so we do not know a lot about it. It is only four to eight inches long. It uses its strong claws and hard nose to push tunnels through the sand. The marsupial mole's golden fur is often

stained red from the sand.

The marsupial mole is blind, so it finds food by listening underground. It eats grubs, worms, caterpillars, lizards, and even centipedes.

The marsupial mole mother's pouch is backward-facing. It does not fill with sand as she digs. Look at that mole go!

Were you ever a pouch baby? No, but you were small and helpless when you were born, too! Human moms feed, hold, and care for their babies as they grow. Just like marsupial moms keep their little pouch babies safe and cozy.